BACCARAT

BACCARAT

EVERYTHING YOU WANT TO KNOW
ABOUT PLAYING AND WINNING

by Tommy Renzoni

The Citadel Press   Secaucus, N.J.

Introduction

FOR THE LAST FORTY-ODD YEARS I HAVE BEEN A professional gambler. I've played all the games—craps, poker, blackjack, you name it—so many times I could probably walk up to a table blindfolded and begin wagering without much of a disadvantage. I have a strong affection for gambling. After all, it has been my life's work. I love all the games. But one is my particular favorite: Baccarat.

I've devoted a major portion of my career to Baccarat, most of the last two decades, in fact. I introduced the game to the United States about a dozen years ago. By now, it is being played in every major casino in Las Vegas, according to my revised rules. It has also been picked up in England, where it is called Punto-Banco—played with my Baccarat rules.

It's my baby, my game. And that's why I think I know enough about Baccarat to tell you what it's

5

all about. I'm also going to try to convince you, whether you're a professional or an amateur, that Baccarat is the most exciting, simple and potentially rewarding game of them all.

By the time you finish reading what I have to say, you will probably be planning a trip to Las Vegas to play Baccarat yourself. And before you turn the last page, you should be well informed enough to do just that. For I'll not only be telling you how the game is played, how it compares to its illustrious parents (Chemin de fer and European Baccarat), the best way to bet at Baccarat and where you can find the Baccarat action in Las Vegas, I'll also be introducing you to some of the fabulous characters who have played the game, many of them at my tables, throughout Baccarat's twelve-year existence in the United States.

Baccarat players like Frank Sinatra, Prince Khashoggi of Saudi Arabia, the Mexican high roller who dresses like an unemployed ditch digger, the South American playboy with the looks of a movie idol and the physique of an olympic athlete, movie mogul Jack Warner, the mysterious and beautiful Chinese woman who draws male players to the table like a queen bee summoning drones—and many others.

Along the way, I'll be telling you a little about myself and my life as a gambler. I was just breaking into the profession in New York City when Arnold Rothstein, Nick the Greek and Joe Gould were at the zenith of their notoriety. I was running a Baccarat table at my friend George Raft's Capri Casino in Cuba when Castro and his rebels came storming out of the hills of Oriente Province and overran Havana. I was there on the opening night of Baccarat at the Sands Hotel in Las Vegas, when the house was alleged to have lost $250,000.

Last but not least, I'll also be revealing the secrets of professional gambling; the principles that professional gamblers live by, swear to, as they play for stakes that often amount to more than most people earn in a decade. What you have to know about each game before you play it. How to manage the money you are gambling with. Which bets to make and which bets to stay away from. How to bet so you stand a chance of winning at least twelve times as much as you might lose. How the pros handle themselves at the gaming tables. Why Baccarat is the simplest and therefore the best game for the weekend gambler to play.

What you are about to read, then, is primarily about the game of Baccarat. But as I have indicated, it is actually much more than that. So much more, in fact, that I'd be willing to give anyone a better than even-money bet that they will find something fascinating in these pages. Come to think of it, I'd be willing to give you twelve to five that after reading this book, even a long-term loser would think twice before saying "you'll never catch me gambling again."

Chapter

One

THE FATHER AND MOTHER OF LAS VEGAS BACCARAT are Chemin de fer and European Baccarat. The best features of each of these games were merged to create a pleasant and exciting contest. Like those two games, the object is to reach a card total of nine or come as close as you can to that number.

The Vegas version of Baccarat, the one I introduced to the United States in the late Fifties, originated in Argentina. Played under a slightly different set of rules there, Baccarat was an offshoot of the much older game of Chemin de fer. Baccarat in South America and the U.S. retains the high-stakes excitement, glamour and distinction of Chemin de fer, which kings and queens risked entire realms over down through history, but they add to that venerable game the purity of sheer chance.

9

European Baccarat, which also grew out of Chemin de fer, is a game of a different stripe. It has about as much relationship to U.S. Baccarat as a whore does to a lady. They are both built the same way, but the tone of their activity is usually quite different. Here's why:

Unlike the European version, there are no options, no decisions for the player to make as the cards are turned up in U.S. Baccarat. A trained monkey could play!

The decision is the player's choice of how much to bet and whether to wager with the bank or with the player. You can bet the minimum—$20 in most houses in Vegas, $5 in two or three—up to the maximum—$2,000 in most places. Caesar's Palace used to allow anyone a $4,000 maximum but now you must ask for it. They allowed Sinatra, Danny Schwartz and other high rollers $8,000 wagers. Sinatra used to complain constantly because they wouldn't allow him $16,000!

Two thousand dollars on your decision. And with the exception of which side you bet, everything is automatic. And the hand takes about as long to play as it took you to read this paragraph! Is it any wonder that Baccarat is considered the most exciting action in the casino?

No skill. You make your bet. The cards are dealt. If Dame Fortune is smiling at you, you win. Or. . . . It's as simple as that.

Baccarat—from now on I'll refer to the U.S. version that way—is played with eight decks of regular playing cards. Depending on the casino, these decks are shuffled by either a croupier, or the players, or both. The cards are then checked by the croupier to see that they are all face down. He mixes them again, and then, in what has become an automatic ritual, one player is asked to cut the 416-card deck.

The cards are then placed in a shoe. For anyone who has never seen one, the shoe is simply a rectangular wooden or plastic box. It is about as wide as a playing card is long. On the upper end, there is an opening through which the cards are inserted. On the lower end, there is a narrow slit through which cards are removed, one at a time, and dealt onto the table.

There are only two hands dealt in Baccarat: a bank hand and a player's hand. While there are only two hands, any number of people can play. The only real limitation is the number of seats at a table and the space surrounding it. From two to sixteen players can sit down to play at a Baccarat table. In addition to the players, there are three croupiers—one calls the cards as they are turned up, and the other two handle the payoffs. There are also one or two observers, who stand or sit on raised platforms back from the table so they can watch the game, settle infrequent disputes and see to it that everything is being handled properly.

The table itself is usually kidney-shaped, from

ten to twelve feet long and three to four feet wide. The kidney-shaped or indented conformation of the table was arrived at to allow a place for the croupiers to stand. From that point they can reach out to handle money or cards anywhere on the table.

Although they vary in size, the usual table seats twelve players. Sometimes when the action calls for it, two tables will be set up by a casino in the same Baccarat room. If conditions are really crowded, on a New Year's weekend, for example, all the seats may be taken up and additional players who stand around the table behind the regular places are also allowed to make bets.

To illustrate how the game is played, let's say that there are twelve players seated at a table. Their places are numbered 1–12. After the shuffling and cutting is completed, player No. 1 receives the shoe. He has become the bank hand. Mind you, he does not even have to bet on the bank hand, the one he is about to deal to himself. In Baccarat, he can bet either way—on the bank hand he deals himself or on the player's hand he deals out. In any case, he deals out four cards from the base of the shoe. One to the player, one to the banker—himself. A second to the player, a second to the banker. (Remember, in Baccarat, there are only two hands dealt during each decision.) Of the remaining eleven players seated at the table, the one who is dealt the player's hand is determined by the amount of money each of them bets against the bank. Whoever bets the highest amount of money against the bank is dealt the player's hand.

Let's say player No. 7 bets more than anyone else at the table against the bank. He becomes the recipient of the player's hand during that one particular decision. Now we have Player No. 1 playing the bank hand and dealing, and Player No. 7 receiving the player's hand. The remaining players —2–6 and 8–12—have already placed bets either that the bank hand will win or the player's hand will win.

All bets, including those by Player No. 7 and Player No. 1 (whether or not the dealer has bet for or against his own bank hand) are now automatically covered by the casino. The banker deals four cards, as previously described. In some decisions, which will be illustrated shortly, an additional card or two may have to be dealt. Whether or not this is true, all betting ends before any cards are pulled from the shoe. From that point on, everyone at the table simply watches as the banker deals and the holder of the player's hand receives. The hand that totals nine or is closest to it wins. Those that bet on the winning hand collect. Those that didn't bet on the winning hand lose their money to the casino.

The shoe and the banker's hand move from left

to right around the table each time the bank hand loses. Whether or not the person dealing has bet for or against it, if the banker's hand loses, the shoe passes from Player No. 1 to Player No. 2; then from Player No. 2 to Player No. 3 when the banker's hand loses again; and so on. Each time a player has the shoe passed to him, he assumes the role of the banker and deals himself the banker's hand. Nonetheless, he can bet either way: on his own banker's hand or on the player's hand. In addition, anyone with the shoe may give it up, pass it along, after *any* decision—in other words even when the bank hand wins—if he so wishes.

When a person receives the shoe, there is a prescribed way for him to deal out the cards. He draws a card for the player—face down—and slides it to the croupier. The croupier in turn places it, again face down, in front of the person receiving the player's hand. The banker then pulls a card for himself and slides it face down beneath the shoe. The procedure is repeated. Now both hands have been dealt. The croupier does not touch the banker's hand at all. The player turns over his cards. Then the banker pulls his two cards out from under the shoe and turns them face up.

At this point, a decision may have been reached in just those four cards, according to the rules of Baccarat as it is played in Las Vegas. If that is the case, the winners collect their bets, which have been faded by the casino, and the losers see their money taken in by one of the croupiers. Often, however, the totals of each individual hand call for a third card to be dealt to the player's hand, the banker's hand, or both, under the automatic rules of the game. In that case, the decision is held up until a fifth, and, possibly, a sixth card are dealt. But never more than six cards are dealt in a single decision. If after four, five or six cards are dealt the decision is a tie, another pair of hands is dealt. Bets in this situation can be pulled off the table, left, changed or increased.

It all sounds a little complicated, if you have never played before, but it isn't really. Not nearly as complicated as poker or the variety of ways you can bet at craps. I will explain and illustrate the automatic rules that govern each hand, each decision and how the money is won or lost. At first glance, those rules may seem complicated too. But they really aren't any more complicated than those that apply to the other games I've mentioned. In fact they are simpler, once you learn them.

Most important, you actually don't have to know how to deal from the shoe, how to handle the player's hand or where to place your bets on the table. The croupiers in any Las Vegas casino will tell you exactly what to do in each case. What's more, they will make sure you collect your money if you win, and by the manner in which they call out the cards as they are dealt and the hands develop, they will be explaining exactly how you win or lose. Like betting that the jockey with the blue colors will beat the one wearing red silks, all you have to do is place your money on the banker's or the player's hand. The croupiers will do all the rest. You don't have to make any decisions—such as whether or not to draw two or three cards as in poker—because the game is entirely automatic. There is only one bet for you to make—before the hands are dealt.

As the hand develops, nobody, including the croupier, decides whether or not the banker's or player's hand must stand or draw an additional card. The automatic rules of the game dictate that. In certain cases, according to the total of the first two cards dealt either hand, the player or the banker must stand. Sometimes both have to. In the same fashion, a different total of the first two cards may dictate that either the player or the banker or both must be dealt an additional card.

No options. No decisions. No skill required. Just an initial choice of which hand to bet on and how much to wager. You pick either the player's hand or the banker's hand. Then you bet anything from the minimum allowed to the house limit. Then you watch the cards as they are dealt and turned over to find out whether you've won or lost. How simple can a game be?

BaccaraT
RULES

PLAYER
HAVING

1-2-3-4-5-10	DRAWS A CARD
6-7	STANDS
8-9 NATURAL	Banker Cannot Draw

BANKER
HAVING

	Draws When Giving	Does Not Draw When 3rd Card Is
3	1-2-3-4-5-6-7-9-10	8
4	2-3-4-5-6-7	1-8-9-10
5	4-5-6-7	1-2-3-8-9-10
6	6-7	1-2-3-4-5-8-9-10
7	STANDS	
8-9	NATURAL - Player Cannot Draw	

PICTURES AND TENS DO NOT COUNT

IF PLAYER TAKES NO CARD
BANKER STANDS ON 6

Chapter

Two

THE RULES CARD ON THE FACING PAGE IS FAIRLY
standard for any of the casinos in Las Vegas where
U.S. Baccarat is played. The same holds true where
the game is offered in England and Europe. Only
the layout of the card varies slightly. The rules
themselves never change in my version of Baccarat and cards like the one shown here contain
all you need to know to sit down at a Baccarat
table.

Compilations of rules, however, quite often lose
a little something when they are compressed to fit
onto a pocket-sized card or pamphlet. Written in
the most terse fashion possible, their terminology
may pose a slight problem for the player who has
never taken part in a particular game. At the
same time, some rules cards for the variety of
games played in Las Vegas can be inadvertently

misleading, because in his effort to compress and shorten the information, a writer may not realize that the brief final sentence he comes up with implies something he never intended to say.

Just the other day, for example, I noticed a rule pamphlet for one of Las Vegas' larger casinos that was more than a bit confusing about a particular type of bet in the game of craps. Now, everyone who has ever played craps in a casino knows what a "place bet" is. You make a bet on the 4, 5, 6, 8, 9 or 10 and if the shooter makes the number you bet on before he throws a 7 and loses the dice, you win. And that goes for any of these six "place bets." In the misleading rules pamphlet I'm talking about, the explanation reads: "If the shooter throws *any of these numbers* before a 7, you win." What the writer meant, of course, was if you bet on any one of these numbers and *it* is thrown before a losing 7, you win. But it turned out sounding like you would win if any of the numbers was thrown, no matter which one of them you bet on.

So for the sake of those who might find the precise rules card a little too terse for comfort, I'm going to spell out each rule and then I'll try to illustrate them individually in an actual playing situation.

The betting is completed and four cards have been dealt out—two for the player, two for the banker. In other words, both the player and the banker "have" two cards. The word "have" is the source of the term "having" on the rules card. Now the rules come into effect. In each hand, the cards will total a number from 0 to 9. (Aces count as one, numbered cards count as their face value —from 2 to 9—10's and picture cards count as 0.)

Bearing in mind that no one may draw a third card if either hand has a "natural" 8 or 9 in the first two cards, let's take a look at the rules that govern the player's hand first:

1) If in those first two cards he has been dealt, the player has a total of 1, 2, 3, 4, 5 or 0 (a ten and a picture card, for example), he draws a card automatically.

2) If in the first two cards he draws a total of 6 or 7, he must stand pat. In other words, he may not draw a card, according to the automatic rules. (In this case, the banker would have to have 7 to beat the player's 6, 8 to beat the player's 7—or 9, of course—after all cards in the decision have been dealt.)

3) As indicated, the player must also stand when he has been dealt an 8 or a 9 in the first two cards. These totals are called "a natural 8" and "a natural 9" when they are dealt in the opening pair of cards to either the banker or the player. They are the second highest and highest hands in Baccarat, respectively, and obviously they are difficult to tie or beat.

And now for the banker:

1) If the banker has dealt himself a total of 3 in those first two cards while dealing the player an 8 on the third card, the dealer may not draw. (In this case, the word "giving" in the rules card is synonymous with "dealing a third card to the player.")

2) Conversely, if the banker has dealt himself a 3 in those first two cards, he automatically must draw if he has given the player any other third card but an 8.

3) If the banker has dealt himself a 4 in the first two cards, he draws if he has dealt the player a 2, 3, 4, 5, 6, or 7 as the third card.

4) If the banker has dealt himself a 4 in the first two cards and has, in turn, given the player a 1, 8, 9, or 0 as a third card, the banker may not draw.

5) If the banker has 5, he draws when he has dealt a third card of 4, 5, 6 or 7 to the player.

6) If the banker has a 5, he may not draw if he has given the player 1, 2, 3, 8, 9 or 0—once again, as the *third* card.

7) If the banker has 6, he must draw if he has given the player a 6 or 7 as the third card. He may not draw if he has dealt the player any other card.

8) If the banker has 7 in the first two cards, he automatically has to stand pat.

9) The banker also has to stand pat (even though this is not specifically stated in the rules card) with 6 if the player does not draw a third card. In other words, when the player has two cards totaling 6, 7 or a "natural" 8 or 9.

By now you're probably wondering what the banker must do according to the automatic rules of U.S. Baccarat if he has a 1, 2 or 0 in his first two cards.

10) In this case he draws no matter what the player has in two *or* three cards—except, of course, a natural 8 or 9. (Like rule number 9, this rule is so automatic and so widely known among Baccarat players that rules card compilers and writers always seem to assume that it doesn't need to be stated.)

You'll notice also that some rules cards stipulate both the player and the banker have to turn their first two cards over if they have a natural 8 or 9. While that is true, the player must always act first in Baccarat. So if he has an 8 or a 9 in the first two cards, he has to turn them over immediately. The banker with an 8 or a 9 doesn't have to display them until the player has turned over his first two cards.

Finally, 9's and 8's in the first two cards ("naturals") win automatically, unless the opposing hand equals or beats them in the total of the first two cards dealt. In other words, if either the player or the banker has a natural 8 or 9, there is no drawing. Automatically, the two hands must stand, and four possibilities arise: The natural 8 or 9 wins because the other hand totals 0 to 7. Two 8's equal one another and the decision is called a "tie." Two 9's equal one another and the decision is also a tie. A natural 9 in one hand beats a natural 8 in the other.

Right about now you're probably thinking, "*Whew,* it's just too much to remember. It's just too complicated." Not really, though, when you consider how many kinds of bets you can make on any given crap table, with odds that vary each time. And don't forget, the dealers or croupiers at any Baccarat table in Las Vegas will be calling out what is happening throughout each decision as it is played, so you really don't have to know any of these rules at all. You just bet your money on the player or the banker, then watch and wait to see and hear when, how and why you've won or lost that particular bet.

You've never played before and the prospect of handling the shoe for the first time makes you nervous? There's nothing to it. You just slide the cards out one at a time. On the cards for the player, you just continue the slide toward the croupier, who handles the player's hand. You deal yourself cards by sliding them out of the shoe— and instead of continuing the slide toward the croupier, you simply stop the card and slide it back under the edge of the shoe. One for the player, one for the banker. Repeat. Listen to the croupier, he'll show you how on your first try. One or two deals and you'll have the knack of it.

Now I'll illustrate a few of the automatic rules in actual playing situations.

The player is dealt a king and an 8, the banker has an ace and 5: Since one hand is a natural, the automatic rules say no drawing is allowed. The player wins, 8 over 6.

The player is dealt a 4 and a 4, banker has a 10 and a 9: Two naturals, no drawing permitted. Banker wins, 9 over 8.

The player is dealt a 6 and a 3, the banker gets a 7 and a 2: Two naturals, no drawing. Tie hand, 9 to 9, and a new hand is dealt. Remember that when a tie develops, all bets on the table, no matter where they have been placed, may be taken off, left, reduced or increased (within house limits) or switched from one hand to the other.

Player has a king and an ace, banker has a 10 and a 3: Player, having 1, must draw (unless the banker has a natural, of course). Player's third card is a 5. Total is 6. Banker having 3 has given a 5, so he must draw. Banker's third card is a 4. Total is 7. Banker wins, 7 to 6.

Player has a 2 and a 3, banker has an ace and a

3: Player, having 5, must draw. His third card is a 4. Total is 9. Banker having 4 and giving a 4 must draw. Banker draws a ten (zero). Player wins, 9 to 4.

Player has a 3 and a 4, banker has a queen and a 5: Player, having a 7, must stand. Banker has 5 and must draw. Banker's third card is a 3. Banker wins, 8 to 7.

Player has a jack and a 2, banker has an ace and a 5: Player, having 2, draws a 4 for a total of 6. Banker having 6 and giving a 4 cannot draw. Tie hand, 6–6.

Player has a 2 and a 3, banker has a 3 and a 3: Player, having 5, draws a 4 for total of 9. Banker, having 6 and giving a 4, may not draw. Player wins, 9 to 6.

Player has a king and a 7, banker has a pair of queens: Player, having 7, must stand. Banker, having 0, must draw. Banker draws an 8. Banker wins, 8 to 7.

Within minutes of watching the Baccarat table at any casino in Las Vegas, all of the foregoing will fall into place easily. The value of each hand will quickly become obvious, and until you know the values and the rules automatically, the croupier will call them out anyway. If you aren't satisfied with that, sit down with a deck of cards and deal out ten Baccarat hands, using this chapter as a guide. By the time you're finished, you'll have it all down pat.

In addition to the rules that govern each hand in Baccarat, there are a few other things to know, all of them easily and quickly absorbed. Baccarat tables are marked in such a way that no one could make the mistake of putting down a bet in the wrong place. There is a section of the green felt table marked off specifically for each of the 12 to 16 chairs that surround it.

Say you're in chair number 3. Immediately in front of you is a section (marked "3") where you can stack your money and place the shoe when it is your turn to be banker. Extending out toward the center of the table is another segment relating to your chair. This segment will be part of a large area marked "PLAYERS." Obviously, that is where you place a bet on the player's hand. Moving further toward the center of the table, another broad area is marked "BANK." This area is also divided up into segments that relate to seat numbers. If you are in seat number 3 and you wish to place a bet on the banker's hand, you put your money up (before the cards are dealt) in the bank segment marked with a "3."

In the middle of the table, directly in front of the croupiers, there are usually two slots. Through one of these, the discards are dropped after each hand, or decision. The other one is a money slot, into which credit markers, unusable old currency and chips from other casinos are dropped.

When you make a wager on the "Player" and you win, you are paid even money on your wager. Thus, a $100 bet is paid off with another $100.

When you make a wager on the "Banker" and win, you are also, seemingly, paid even money. Except that the house charges you five percent of the amount wagered. Thus, if you bet $100 and win, you are paid another $100—but tokens indicating that you owe the house five dollars are placed in the box in front of the croupiers. As this debt mounts up, the total is called to your attention. The house prefers to collect its vigorish before it adds up to too much money. In the case of high rollers, it will, however, grant the player the courtesy of waiting until the shoe is exhausted before collecting commissions. When the shoe is finished, all commissions are collectable.

Does this mean that the house makes five percent on all money wagered? Obviously not. It makes no commission on player bets. Nor does it collect anything on tie bets.

There has been much controversy about what percent the house has going for it. Even the so-called "experts" quarrel on this score.

The best bet in craps with the shooter is a flat bet on the pass line. The house percentage is 1.41.

Although some people claim that the house percentage in Baccarat is only .085, I happen to believe that it is closer to 1.25. In other words, of all the money bet at a table, the house will eventually collect one and a quarter percent.

If that doesn't sound like much, you're not a good mathematician. For example, if the average wager is only $300 and there are twelve players at a table, there is $3,600 wagered. In time, the house will collect $45. No more than a couple of minutes are consumed with each hand.

But take a big money table where some players are wagering the maximum $2,000 on the turn of a card. Let us say that $12,000 is bet on each hand. The house now can count on eventually collecting $150. Multiply this by thirty or more hands dealt in an hour and you have a gross profit for the house of close to $5,000 an hour.

Last April, the Del Webb casinos did a computer study of the results of many thousands of games.

The casinos determined that they were making 1.16 percent on "bank" bets and 1.26 percent on "player" bets. On tie bets (some tables offer 9 for 1 odds against a tie) the house earns 14.36 percent.

It is obvious then that the proposition bets are sucker bets—not unlike the "field bet" at the crap table. Avoid them.

And keep in mind the reality that the longer you stay at any casino table, the greater the probability you will be ground out.

When you are lucky, ride with the streak for all the dollars you can gather in. But when the streak turns, leave the table as soon as you are sure it has turned.

Never worry about keeping track of the five percent charge on your winning bets on the banker's hand. A money-handling croupier keeps track of this charge for you when you bet on the banker's hand and win. He places chips or markers indicating how much you owe the casino in a small square or rectangle marked with your seat number. This section of the table is marked clearly and is located in the middle, directly in front of the croupiers.

This five percent charge is neither here nor there. If you're going to gamble in a casino, where the games are always mechanically in favor of the house one way or another over the long run, you might as well play Baccarat. In addition to being an exciting game with the highest limits in Las Vegas, Baccarat offers you a chance to play where no skill at cards or knowledge of the rules is required. Baccarat also presents the most reasonable built-in, or automatic, "house-edge" anywhere in the United States.

Few players know what they're up against, percentage-wise, when they play the slot machines. But the figure is so astronomical that anyone thinking about it would have to be crazy to play the slots for anything but enjoyment. The same goes for Keno. While they are not nearly as high as those working against you at a slot machine or in Keno, the house percentage you buck while playing blackjack, roulette or craps don't compare favorably with the odds in Baccarat either. With one or two betting exceptions in craps, that is. (Poker is not considered a mechanical casino game since most casinos simply rent rooms where it can be played privately for a flat fee.)

But don't take my word for it. Listen to what John Scarne, the man some people call America's foremost authority on gambling, has to say in *Scarne's Complete Guide to Gambling:*

"If you still insist on casino gambling after having read this book, and you find yourself in a casino that harbors all the standard casino games . . . and you would like to give yourself the best possible chance to win, sit yourself down at the Baccarat table."

Chapter

Three

SINCE THEY ARE DIRECTLY RELATED, BACCARAT AND its foreign cousins have many similarities. For one thing, the table used for all games is pretty much the same. And while six decks are often used to fill the shoe, or sabot, in Chemin de fer, rather than the eight for Baccarat, the object of the game is the same: a total of 9 in two or three cards, or as close to it as possible. The hands are dealt the same way in Chemin de fer and Baccarat, and usually the number of hands—two—remains the same. I say usually, because there is a version of Chemin de fer called Double Tableau in which there are two players' hands.

In Chemin de fer the active player or person dealt the player's hand, is the one who has bet the most against the bank, just as in Baccarat. But there ends the similarity between U.S. Baccarat (which is now played in only a few other places in the world) and Chemin de fer, Double Tableau and European-style Baccarat.

There are four basic differences between U.S. Baccarat and its foreign relatives. These differences are in the areas of banking, betting, possession of the shoe and the rules.

In Double Tableau and European Baccarat, for example, the shoe and the bank remain stationary —in the hands of the house or casino. The players may bet on either player's hand but not on the bank.

The players are permitted to bet the bank hand if they wish to in Chemin de fer. If they win on the bank hand they are charged five percent by the house. The players can bet on the single player's hand in European Baccarat, or select one of the two player's hands in Double Tableau. No matter which way they bet or how often they win or lose, the players never get the shoe or bank. That remains in the hands of a house croupier.

In some European casinos, a group of people will buy the bank concession—in other words take over the banking of the game. Obviously, it takes quite a bit of money to swing such a move. For not only do the bets have to be covered by the concessionaires, but approximately fifty percent of their monthly take must be turned over to the casino for the privilege of banking the game.

In Chemin de fer, the shoe, or banker's hand, rotates as it does in U.S. Baccarat, but the house or casino does not bank the game with its own money. Instead, the players at the table fade each other's bets and the house simply collects the standard five percent of winning banker's hand bets as a charge for the privilege of playing and using the casino's equipment. In Chemin de fer, for example, if a man has the shoe and wants to bet $10,000, he may do so if any or all of the players at the table with him will cover that amount of money. The hitch is that if the players only want to fade $1,000 of the banker's bet, that is all the banker can wager.

Another difference in Chemin de fer is that usually the banker bets his own hand (until he loses a pass or decision) and the players bet against him. Their money rides on the player's hand. Occasionally, if there is enough money and enthusiasm among the players, a banker may allow someone without the shoe to fade an additional amount being bet against his hand. But this is a decision that is strictly up to the banker.

The most significant difference between U.S. Baccarat (which is called Punto Banco in London and the few other places around the world where it is played) and its foreign relatives involves the rules of the game. While there are absolutely no options in U.S. Baccarat, there *are* in Double

35

Tableau, European-style Baccarat and Chemin de fer.

These options, which are just about the same in all three games, may not seem important at first glance, but they are. For when a game is automatic, where every coup, or play a player or banker makes is dictated by the rules and the cards as they are turned up, no skill is required to play. Since neither the banker nor the player in U.S. Baccarat has a choice, in any situation, about whether or not to draw a card or stand (as he would in blackjack, for example) neither has an advantage over the other.

The options in the other versions of the game involve both the player and the banker. There are only three of them, but they spell the difference between a game of skill and judgment (which many weekend gamblers would do well to stay away from) and a game of pure chance. The options are:

1) A player having a total of 5 in two cards may either stand or draw. (In U.S. Baccarat, he automatically gets a third card.)

2) A banker having 3 who has given a 9 to the player in three cards may either stand or draw. (In U.S. Baccarat, he *must* draw if he has 3 and gives a 9.)

3) A banker having 5 may draw or stand if he

has given the player 4 on the third card. (In U.S. Baccarat, he must draw in this situation.)

Three seemingly innocuous options. But they are far from that. Since there is an option to do one thing or another in the situations cited, it is imperative that the cards remain face down longer than they do in U.S. Baccarat. Long enough, that is, for a player or banker to make his decision about the option that has become available. And that decision, which must be based on skill—acquired knowledge of the game and the way the cards tend to go, awareness of the percentages for and against drawing or standing in a given situation—dictates that either the player or the banker will have a natural advantage each time an option arises. It stands to reason that one or the other will have more skill, judgment or acquired knowledge. If it doesn't happen to be the active player, all the other players betting with him are stuck because they have to depend on his judgment. If the banker has the option, but not the skills required for it, his bet is jeopardized.

In the case of Double Tableau and European Baccarat, where the shoe or bank never changes hands, it follows that the players will be at something of a disadvantage in most cases when an option arises because a croupier or house banker will undoubtedly have played the game many more times than all but a few of the players he faces. The house man will therefore tend to have more experience, more knowledge, skill and good judgment in an option-available situation. After all, the man is a professional!

All of which leads me back to the significant advantages, for players of all levels, of U.S. Baccarat.

First and most important, there are no options. Therefore, knowledge of the game, skill and judgment are unnecessary. The automatic rules take care of those factors for everyone. There are, of course, professional techniques of betting (at any game) that I will come to. In other words, skill, knowledge and judgment one can acquire and apply in managing the money he or she gambles with to the best advantage. And knowledgeable money management *can* mean the difference between winning and losing in any game, including Baccarat. But as far as skill, knowledge and judgment relating to playing the game itself are concerned, forget them. They are not needed. No one, professional or amateur, casino employee or private gambler, can influence the outcome of a decision in Baccarat, Vegas-style, with any of those otherwise precious personal resources.

In blackjack, as in Chemin de fer, there are frequent occasions when a player must decide whether he should stand or draw. Those decisions affect the outcome of every hand that is dealt. Obviously, to cite the most salient example, a raw amateur without the knowledge to stand when he has a 16 or 17 in a game of blackjack, is up against terrible odds because of his lack of skill and judgment. The same rank amateur can sit down at a Baccarat table, and because he has no options, because the rules *dictate* every play, he will never find himself in the same situation. The rules *force* him to play in the most advantageous way. Likewise, a casino that the rank amateur is playing against never has a choice or an option that might give it the slightest edge. Banker and dealer must stand or draw when the rules call for it. Thus, in Baccarat, the amateur as well as the professional is simply bucking pure chance.

If that were not enough of a lure for Baccarat, consider the additional advantages:

Since the casino banks, or fades, all the bets in Baccarat, no crowd of people is required for a game. If there are not enough players available, the house will station one, two, three or four employees at the table to act as players. Thus a single gambler with an itch to play Baccarat can come in at any hour and play as long as he wishes to. Because the participants fade each other in Chemin de fer, it sometimes takes hours to find enough people with enough money to make a game worthwhile.

In Baccarat, the player can bet either way—on the banker's hand or the player's. Imagine yourself betting the player's hand and not having much luck. You decide you'd like to try betting the other way. (Many people do and often find it rewarding.) You can do it in Baccarat, but you can't in any of the game's foreign relatives.

Because the house covers all bets in Baccarat, a person with an urge to gamble a lot of money can find satisfaction. Casino funds are relatively unlimited when it comes to fading your bets. So you can gamble for as much money as you'd like to —$2,000 at a time. The same doesn't hold true in Chemin de fer, because few groups of players who hire a table and sit down to play have the funds to match those a casino has available. So the game can't possibly last as long or involve as much money.

At one time or another, all the foreign relations of Baccarat were played in Las Vegas. Chemin de fer had the most staying power. And for some reason, it was decades before anyone brought the advantages of my version of Baccarat to the attention of both players and casinos in Vegas. But somebody finally did and I happened to be the lucky person. You should have seen how quickly the owners of Las Vegas' biggest operations and the players they cater to adopted my baby when I finally arranged her debut.

Chapter

Four

BACCARAT DRAWS ALL KINDS OF PEOPLE, FROM HAY-
seeds who have never bet or even seen big money
before, to celebrities, high rollers and degenerate
gamblers who win and lose tens of thousands of
dollars at a sitting. I've had someone standing outside the Baccarat room motion me over and ask
me if that was stage money—make-believe, monop-
oly-style scrip—the players were betting.

"Where you from?" I asked the guy.

"Outside Louisville, Kentucky," he answered.

It must have been quite a ways outside, con-
sidering the fact that big money is bet around
Louisville—and I don't mean just at the Derby
—all the time. I glanced over at the table and
noticed the bets added up to maybe ten thousand
dollars. By Baccarat standards, that wasn't even
half the amount that could have been wagered if

all twelve players had bet the house limit of two thousand. "Haven't you ever seen any real money?" I asked.

"Yeah," the guy said, breaking into his sentence with a long, low whistle. "But not *that* much money."

Here was a guy who must have been forty years old and ten thousand looked like the Bank of England to him. All he'd have to do is watch the Baccarat table over a period of time and it would soon take more than a hundred century notes to make an impression on him.

The fact is, even though $20 bills (the minimum bet in most casinos) are the most common greenbacks you'll see most of the time, quite often, particularly on big holiday weekends, twenties are as scarce as ice cubes along the equator. On those nights, it'll be fifties and hundreds. We often used $500 and $1000 bills when the limit-bettors were clustered around. When they're playing, you witness a night when money in the millions changes hands. Those are the Baccarat players who play—sometimes for hours at a time—and lose or win from $50,000 to $300,000 *each*.

Although the average player can come in almost anytime and bet the minimum as much as he wants to, Baccarat is basically a big money game, a game where someone can play for the highest stakes available—legally—anywhere in the United

States. Now that sort of game automatically draws a wide variety of people with two extremely strong characteristics: they want to gamble rather than just play and they are, in their own way, extremely individualistic, magnetic personalities.

Take Prince ~~Adam~~ Khashoggi of Saudi Arabia, for example. He came up to the rope on a busy night one time, no fuss, no loud flourishes and just waited there—a man who could probably snap his fingers and have almost anything he wanted back home—until I spotted him. The table was crowded, but he'd been in before and I knew he was a big money player, so I went over and arranged for him to have a seat immediately.

When that guy sat down, the atmosphere at the table—even the attitude of the croupiers—changed very quickly. It was almost as if the Prince brought along a high-powered battery and plugged it into the table, the floor and all the chairs. You got a sort of chill looking at him, this very quiet, swarthy-skinned little man who dressed expensively but conservatively. He had the best taste in continental clothing I've ever seen. I'd say he was about forty, very distinguished looking, like a diplomat. But right in the middle of all that reserve there'd be those steel grey eyes of his—the eyes of a man you knew had been up on mountain ranges hunting things. And if the eyes didn't get you, you'd have the knowledge that this man had

43

$300,000 worth of credit—or more—in every casino in town, and was willing to lose all of it in an attempt to win big.

Sometimes he'd come to the table with his wife —a very attractive woman—and we'd bend the rules a little. He'd start betting the limit right off —and so would she, with *his* money, of course. So instead of a limit of $2,000, the Prince would have a $4,000 limit going for him through two separate bets.

When he came, usually after dinner, he came to *gamble*. No short stretches for him. On this particular night, he just kept at it for hours. Finally, early the next morning, after I sent all the help home, after all the other players—including the Princess—had gone to bed, I sat down and played head to head with him. He must have gone through $200,000 by the time we quit around dinner time the following night. It had been up and down, but overall, the cards had gone my way. It could have turned out the other way too. On a number of occasions—the Prince came in about three or four times a year—I'd seen him win $100,000 to $200,000.

You almost never see anyone carrying that kind of money—at least it's not the usual case. People who bet those amounts deal in credit, then reimburse the house for chips they've lost. Obviously, you'd have to have a pretty good balance sheet for any casino to extend itself the way they do for Prince Khashoggi.

Still, there are a lot of people who bet in the $50,000 and up, high-roller category. Frank Sinatra is right up there with the best of them. He's stayed away from Vegas since the highly publicized scuffles he got into with two people over extending his credit limit. But when Sinatra was appearing here, he'd always come into the Baccarat room. I think it's fair to say he liked Baccarat as well as he liked any game. Probably more.

Sinatra rarely played just for fun. He liked gambling. It seemed to relax him. But when he sat down, it was more the gambler gambling than the entertainer gambling for enjoyment. I've seen him win and lose between $50,000 and $100,000 in a single night. Frank's only problem—really the thing that led to his saying goodbye to Vegas for good—was he wanted his own way.

Now understand me, Frank is a gentleman, a very decent person. A lot nicer than many people would have you believe. I know of many things he's done for people, organizations, that needed help. And most of the time, almost *all* the time, he'd do things without any publicity attached to them. Simply out of kindness and charity. But as I said, he wanted his way.

Sinatra was like a magnet at the Baccarat table. Often celebrity friends like Sammy Davis, Jr.,

Peter Lawford, Richard Conte and Dean Martin would be with him. But even when he was playing alone, the air would be charged. Outside the rope that separates the Baccarat room from the rest of the casino, there'd invariably be more than a dozen beautiful women, just watching, just standing there so they could say that they'd been *that* close to Frank.

Lots of times it would be that way whenever any celebrity played. People would just want to play or watch Lucille Ball or Edward G. Robinson when they were at the table. Many other celebrities played at my table at The Sands. In addition to the ones I've mentioned, none of which, by the way, were in Sinatra's class when it came to high rolling, there were Rowan and Martin, Steve Lawrence and his wife, Eydie Gorme, Dionne Warwicke and Don Adams, the comedian, just to name a few. Most of the time, these people just played to pass the time, for enjoyment. But they always brought an added excitement to the game when they were there.

Occasionally, one or another of the celebrities would do something that would add a little anecdote to the colorful history of Baccarat's first dozen years in Vegas. Once, a group of male entertainers—all close friends—had made a swing through a casino playing roulette, craps and blackjack, but for some reason they had skipped or overlooked the Baccarat table. Each one of them had a lovely young girl with him, and they went on up to one suite for what was bound to be one of the biggest blasts of all time. They ordered food and drinks and everything was all set when the ringleader of this particular pack of pals suddenly sat up on his bed and said: "Hey, we never played any Baccarat. A trip to Vegas isn't complete until you've played a little Baccarat."

He got up and put on his shoes again. "Let's go," he said.

"What about the, uh, girls," one of his buddies asked.

"We'll give them cab money—and a little extra —and send them home."

"What . . . about, uh, all this food," the slightly disappointed friend threw in as a last hope.

"They can take it home with them."

The girls were packed out into the hallway with the food and in the process, made enough noise for someone to complain. They were gone by the time one of the house detectives came marching down the carpeted hallway. By this time, the friends had all gone to their rooms, spruced up a little and were back in the ringleader's suite. They were about to leave for the casino when someone noticed one of the girls was still there—hiding in the bathroom, naked as a suckling pig.

"I don't want to go," she said.

No one ever relayed what the ringleader said to her. But the gist of it was easily understood by the house detective as he came to within about thirty feet of the room. Out came the girl, still naked and squealing at the top of her lungs. She landed on the carpet in a position familiar to most gynecologists. Then the door slammed behind her. This stopped the detective dead in his tracks. He was trying to figure out how he was going to get this howling, naked chickie downstairs and out through the main lobby to a cab, without causing a riot, when the door to the room opened again and the girl's clothes came flying out like so many broken balloons.

Such is the lure of Baccarat.

For the most part, however, celebrities generate most of their excitement just by playing. Men like Jack Warner, the film mogul; Henry Ford (I only remember seeing him play once); Mario Puzo, the author of *The Godfather;* and others like them are luminous attractions at a Baccarat table. People can't seem to control the urge to play when these individuals are sitting in at Baccarat.

Most of the celebrities are, as I've said, conservative, basically pleasure players. A few of them, however, fit right in with the pros and the high rollers. Like Sinatra, Jack Warner unquestionably fits into this category. He's a short, dapper little man with a trim mustache. I'd say he's in his seventies but he doesn't show it. He has the eyes of an eagle and the courage of a man forty years younger.

You couldn't let him bet enough money. He'd bet more than the house limits at anything he played if you let him. He was always able to get credit of a couple of hundred thousand, and he'd start betting it, as much at a time as he could. He didn't play as often as Prince Khashoggi, but when he did I would say that he'd win and lose just as much.

The greatest high roller I've ever seen wasn't a celebrity at all. He pals around with celebrities and is a friend, an associate of Sinatra's, but back home in San Francisco, Danny Schwartz is the owner of a big construction company. Schwartz is a guy in his forties, short, a very nice dresser. You wouldn't think he's the type of gambler he is by looking at him, but when he plays, you sure know it. He had credit at all the casinos as high as anyone I know of. Over $300,000 in each place. I've heard of him getting as much as a half million in credit at a casino during a visit to Vegas.

I've seen and heard of Schwartz winning and losing three or four hundred thousand. And I've known him to do some very generous things, wild things at a Baccarat table. A limit bettor right from the first hand, Schwartz was playing one night with a party that included Nancy Sinatra, Henry Fonda and his wife and three other show business couples. That night Schwartz bet $4,000 each for Fonda and his wife and the other three pairs, and about $28,000 for Nancy. They all won and tried to give Schwartz back his money. He just smiled and put his hands in his pockets and turned away.

Sometimes, you really can't tell when someone is a high roller the first time they walk in. Willie Budit, a little guy from Mexico City, used to come in looking like an everyday common laborer. Not dirty, but just a pair of Sears and Roebuck slacks and an open shirt—and the face of a hod carrier. He didn't look as if he had enough to pay cab fare back to the airport. But when he started betting, it was the limit, right off the shoulder, immediately.

Eduardo Sabel was an entirely different case. He looked like he should be out on the tennis court, teaching some young lady how to hit a backhand. He was a young man from Peru in his early thirties. Tall, handsome enough to be a movie idol, with the physique of a superstar athlete. He was dark-haired and wore the best, most exclusively tailored clothes you could find anywhere in the world. He always came alone to Vegas, but by the time he'd gotten unpacked, there seemed to be a harem of beautiful women with him. At first glance, you might think he was a playboy. But when he sat down at the Baccarat table, you knew he was there for serious gambling.

Sabel was what we call a rough gambler. Money was no object to him. He stood to win all the money he could, and he would play and keep on playing until he won or lost $100,000. Like the Prince, Sabel would often bring someone with him —usually a woman—to bet an extra $2,000 of his money on each decision. Sabel was right up there with the best of them, the highest rollers.

In addition to the Sabels, the Princes, the Jack Warners, all kinds of people played. Sometimes someone from Nebraska, a farmer maybe, would come in. You'd never seen him before, never see him again. But that night he would sit down and win or lose between ten and twenty thousand.

Professional gamblers would come in too, some of whom I've known for twenty, thirty years. Professional sports figures, business executives, you name it. There are even a few hotel owners and operators who play high stakes Baccarat during their off-hours. All of them, from the Prince right on down to the Nebraska farmer or someone just up from L. A. for the weekend with a hundred or more to have fun gambling with, go into the game with the same odds going against them, the same chance of winning. Because as I've pointed out, there is no knowledge, no skill involved in Baccarat.

Obviously, someone who goes in with $50,000 to gamble has a chance of winning a lot more money because his average bets are higher. But if you go in with $500 and you walk away with $1,500, you've done the same thing—percentage-wise—as the guy with the $50,000 bankroll who walks away with $150,000.

Of all the serious players I've mentioned, most were notable for the amount of money they would gamble with. Occasionally, however, I'd run across someone who would bet that kind of money but in a way that distinguished him from the rest. A different style, a separate set of idiosyncrasies or characteristics. One player like that was a multi-millionaire named Murphy, who used to come into the Baccarat room carrying a briefcase. He'd sit down and open the damn thing up and inside he'd have a ham sandwich in wrinkled, reused cellophane and anywhere from $100,000 to $300,000 in neatly stacked bills. On one of his trips to Vegas he won $300,000 at one casino, got in a cab with his newly-filled briefcase, went to another casino, sat down, opened the briefcase up and proceeded to lose everything he'd won.

There was also a New York book publisher who cut quite a figure. A heavyset man, he had a full black beard, which in itself is unusual at a Baccarat table. You just don't see many people with beards playing. This fellow was a fabulous gambler. He'd come out here, sometimes, on an office vacation trip and he'd come out here, sometimes, on an office vacation trip and he'd bring his whole staff. He'd give them money to bet with. If they lost that and went into their own cash, you'd see him playing Baccarat or shooting craps to win them back their money.

I understand the law of averages has caught up with him, but for a time, he couldn't lose at anything he played. The management of one casino used to wince when he walked in the door, he'd beaten them so often. He seemed to be instinctive. I'd see him switch his bets in Baccarat just at the right moment and continue on a fantastic winstreak. I've been told that he would call odds-against-you proposition bets while a pair of dice was still in the air on the way to the end of the table and win those long shots time after time.

He was a very prepossessing figure at the Baccarat table. He would draw other players in with his personality and style—despite the fact that he really didn't look like a gambler, at least not the lean, mean stereotype most people think of—and he would lend the table a wild excitement.

I remember one occasion when the hour had grown late and my staff was exhausted—and looked it. All the other players had departed, but he asked if we would deal one more shoe. He overcame their tiredness very quickly.

"If I win this hand, $1,000 of the winnings is for the dealers!" he announced.

Did that crew suddenly wake up!

He won. "Do you want it as a tip or should I bet it for you?" he asked.

It was a tormenting decision.

"Bet it!" one of the boys said. The others agreed.

Although he played both ways, like Ira Gershwin, the publisher tended to favor the player. He'd been winning with player bets. Now he suddenly switched. You could almost hear the mental groans.

The player showed a 3. The bank had 5. Third card for the player was a 4, making 7. Third card for the bank was a 3, making 8. Bank wins 8 over 7.

A two thousand dollar tip! It was a happy crew that went home that night.

On other occasions, the publisher would send his daughter, Sandy, to the table with $2,000 in her hand. This beautiful, dark-haired, dark-eyed, long-legged girl in her early twenties would casually walk up to an otherwise lackluster table and call a $2,000 wager.

In a minute the decision was made. Then, more often than not, she'd pick up the winnings and just leave, walking across the crowded casino to the elevators with $4,000 in hundreds almost spilling out of her cupped hands.

I saw my share of high rollers while I was in Cuba, too. Men like Chili Mendoza and Pedro Suarez, two fellows who were neck deep in construction contracts with the Batista government, measured up to all the high rollers I've mentioned. The wildest, most spectacularly courageous gambler I ever knew in Cuba, maybe in my entire life, was a fellow named Analito Batisti. Spelled like the dictator but ending with an "i." Analito was on the other side of the gambling tables, by which I mean he was an operator, an owner. He had the Saville Biltmore Hotel in Havana and another private club while I was there, and from time to time I ran Baccarat games for him. The reason why I say he was a spectacular gambler is that he let people play, at all times, with no limit. He'd cover any bet you could make. You can't imagine the amounts of money that were won and lost at his tables. Someone would come in and bet $100,000 on a Baccarat decision, or a spin of the roulette wheel. Analito wouldn't even bat an eye. He'd just nod and the dealers or croupiers would fade the bet.

In situations like that, degenerate gamblers— people to whom gambling has become a compulsion, a part of their life that overshadows everything else including their last shreds of intelligence and common sense—become more noticeable than they are in Vegas. The stakes are so much higher the phenomenon just becomes that much more obvious. But you come across degenerate gamblers, people who gamble foolishly, who do the wrong things to get money to gamble, people who are ruining their lives, in Vegas, too.

The worst case of gambling degeneracy that I can recall in my years at The Sands was a man named Arthur De Bovoise. He was one of the owners of an armored car company in the east. He did some peculiar things on his way to oblivion. He lost constantly, so he began thinking of wrinkles that might possibly change his luck. He started coming into the game with a beautiful woman on his arm, as if that might change things. He'd bet an extra $1,000 for the Salvation Army, or $500 for a casino security guard he liked.

Sometimes De Bovoise would bet his money for someone who wasn't even in the casino, maybe not even in Vegas. He had no sense of controlling his losses—the key to gambling, really. No sense about what he was doing at the table. It got to the point where he was just giving his money away. For some reason, he was a totally self-destructive individual. He wound up owing gambling debts reported to be in the millions of dollars. Finally, it got to be too much for him and he killed himself.

I classify De Bovoise as a degenerate player

because he would play day and night without a thought for food or rest. People like him couldn't care less about entertainment. He'd play all over town, going from one casino to another, just betting and losing, betting and losing. By the end of a night, he'd have blown close to a quarter of a million.

There are other kinds of degenerate players. People who gamble with the wrong kind of money. One of them was Eddie Gilbert, the young fellow who embezzled his family-owned company back east for an enormous amount of cash. A lot of it went down the drain here in Vegas, and then some. He bet hundreds of thousands of dollars at Baccarat, not to mention similar amounts, I'm told, at other games.

He occupied a penthouse suite at The Sands, with a stock market ticker-tape machine at the side of his bed. He'd only been out here off and on for a period of three or four months when they caught up with him. The newspapers and newsmagazines had his picture plastered all over the front pages—along with headlines that told about millions that had been taken. By that time he was already in Brazil. His company wasn't the only outfit that got hit hard. From what I understand, he owed The Sands alone about $130,000 when the authorities started hunting for him.

There have been others who have abused their

credit in Vegas. There's a young lawyer from San Francisco who got carried away after a lucky streak at the International Hotel. He won $90,000, then came over to The Sands and lost every penny of it. He kept on losing as he went from hotel to hotel trying to win the money back. I think he took off owing different casinos $50,000 to $60,000 each all over town. I believe they're still looking for him.

Sometimes you just can't understand why a particular person will do the crazy things they do to gamble big money. One fellow had everybody in Vegas fooled until it turned out he was getting his money the wrong way. This fellow was a gentleman at all times. He won respect, confidence and most important, high credit, wherever he turned up. He was such a sweet, trusting and trustable guy, you never would have guessed what his secrets were. Everybody loved him.

The first time he showed up in Vegas, he had some difficulty getting credit established. He was from out of state, and he was working for an association of civic officials, through which the Federal Government would send economic aid funds for different cities. That first night, he had two cashier's checks from his bank in a west coast city. They were for $50,000 apiece. Well, people in Vegas know that even cashier's checks can be forged or stolen and passed off by somebody other than the payee. Anyway, no one at this particular casino would cash them, since it was a weekend and there was no way to call the bank for verification.

The guy had quite a bit of cash on him, so he played Baccarat with that. On Sunday afternoon, he went over to the manager of the Baccarat table and handed him the checks. "You hold on to these until I get back next weekend," the guy said. "You can check them out tomorrow morning, and then when I get back, we'll talk about my credit line in this place."

Next morning, the manager called the bank and, sure enough, the checks were good. In fact, the bank executive told him, they would have been solid if they were eight to ten times the total of $100,000. So the manager hung up the phone and only then did he notice that the fellow who left the checks had endorsed both of them. Can you believe that? A hundred thousand dollars and the guy leaves it with somebody he's only known for a couple of days.

The manager put the checks in the hotel safe for the guy, and just like he said, he came back the next weekend, and of course, he had no trouble getting credit in six figures from then on anywhere in Vegas. He'd come in to gamble every couple weeks. Sometimes he'd win $100,000 at Baccarat, other times he'd lose the same amount.

In the long run, he went through about $1,000,000. But while he was doing it, he established himself as one of the best-liked people ever to come to Vegas.

I don't mean he enjoyed that reputation—almost legendary, people still talk about him—because he lost a million. He was just one of the nicest human beings you'd ever want to meet. One time, he met these two stewardesses on a plane coming into Vegas. The girls—they couldn't have been more than nineteen or twenty—had another leg of the flight to make, but he handed them plane fare to fly back to Vegas and meet him at one of the casinos. He said he wanted to show them a good time.

The young girls were from Oklahoma. Fresh as cow's milk and green as grass. Instead of just taking off with the money, they flew back to Vegas a couple hours later and came to meet him. He was playing Baccarat by now, so he sat them down and put $1,000 in twenties in front of each of them. Well, they didn't know what to do. They didn't comprehend what was going on. They'd never seen that much money, so they just sat there. Finally, the guy told them it was their money to play with, and they started playing. Pretty soon, he noticed that one of them was mesmerized by a fur coat a woman at the table had draped over a chair.

"You like that?" the guy asked, and the two wide-eyed girls, as slow as Little Annie Fanny, just said, "Uh, huh."

"Charlie," the guy said to the manager of the Baccarat table, "take these girls into the hotel shop and buy them each any fur coat they want. Here's a signed blank check."

Well, it was the good taking care of the innocent. The girls went into the shop and the saleslady started pushing all those $7,000 and $8,000 long mink coats at them. No, they said, they didn't like the long ones. They each wanted one of those "shortie" mink jackets. More stylish. The two kids were so innocent and so bowled over by all this generosity, they never thought for a second that if they took the long coats, they could sell them, buy the jackets and still be about $6,000 ahead.

The "shortie" coats was what they got, and they were wearing them when they came back to the Baccarat table. Just about then, it started to dawn on them that maybe they'd have to *do* something for all the cash and fur. By the time this guy got finished playing, it was plain to see that they were worried. They'd lost the $1,000 apiece, they were wearing the fur jackets, and the guy was ready to go. So one of them got up the nerve to ask him, "What do we have to do for all this?"

Everybody at the table looked up, and naturally, they were all smiling. As nice a guy as he was, nobody expected the answer he gave them. "Nothing, little sweethearts," the guy said. "You made me feel comfortable, at home on an airplane for the first time in my life. And I just wanted to repay you."

With that, he handed each of them a $100 bill and said, "You go on now, and catch the next plane. Don't stick around this town at this hour of the morning or else you might run into somebody who's up to no good."

You're right if you think that made everybody at the table sit up and take notice, everybody's jaw dropped about a minute after the girls went swishing out of the casino in their new mink jackets. The guy had watched them go, and as soon as they were out of sight, he turned to a young hard-looking woman sitting on a lounge chair across the casino, walked over and talked to her for a minute. She got up and followed him on his way back to his room. Only then did the people he'd been playing with realize it was one of the town's veteran hookers, a girl nicknamed Terrible Terry.

So it was a surprise, a shock, to everyone when it was discovered that this guy had somehow or other figured out a way to take a lot of those Federal checks that were earmarked for different cities and deposit them into his own account. While the government was investigating the case, a lot of people in Vegas, casino employees, were called in for questioning. The government was trying to trace where some of the money had gone. I guess they figured they could get some of it back if they could find out where this guy had gambled.

Everybody figured that under this kind of pressure, the guy would crack. But it turned out that he refused to name a single person, a single casino where he'd gambled. He told the judge at his trial that he was the one guilty of wrongdoing and he wanted to pay his debt to society himself. He said that no one in Vegas had known the source of the money he had gambled with, and that no one should be penalized because of it. Not even to the extent of taking the money back from a casino. By the time he was sentenced. I think he had even the judge sorry for having to send him to prison. In any case, I know what people think about him in Vegas. He's out now, on parole. And I'd be willing to give odds that if he ever comes back to Vegas, they'd take up a collection of $100 bills just to help him get back on his feet again.

Strangely enough, of all the high rollers I've seen in my time, the women among them have been scarce. The most memorable woman Baccarat player I can recall is an Oriental lady from L. A. named Irene Lynn. She ran a string of beauty shops, I think. Married to a dentist. She was always an incredible attraction at the Baccarat table.

In her late forties I would guess, but *extremely* well preserved, as the saying goes. But it was her hair that made her stand out so spectacularly. Every night she played it would be a different color. One night she'd have green hair, another, blonde. The next time you saw her it would be purple. It was a sight few people had ever seen before, and even though she was obviously just wearing a series of wigs and falls she owned, the combination of the crazy color and her beauty created a lot of attention—and increased the activity at the Baccarat table.

Women, it seems to me, have always made a positive difference at a gaming table. I don't want to get Freudian about it, but there seems to be a connection between gambling and sex. There's an excitement, a thrill about gambling, particularly when you're winning, that finds its only parallel in sexual love. Women always seem to drift into an area where a big winning streak is going on or where there is a celebrity playing. And they add to the excitement by just being there. If a beautiful woman is actually playing at a Baccarat table, or in any other game, for that matter, time and time again you'll see the activity at the table increase, the number of more substantial bettors grow.

There would have to be something to this theory, because every casino I've ever heard of will have good-looking female employees, shills, sitting at a gaming table playing with house money because they attract male players. They make the room more colorful, beautify it, but basically, they are there as a lure.

You don't have to worry about those good-looking shills, though. They only sit at a table when the house is not busy and the management wants to give things a boost. At a Baccarat table, these house shills make automatic bets of a modest amount of money—most of the time on the player's hand, except when they have the shoe. Then they bet on the bank. But they don't affect the decisions in any way, they have no influence over the way you bet (unless you happen to want to wager with or against them for your own reasons), so they are nothing to be troubled about. The only thing they are placed there for is to attract men to the table, which isn't even necessary ninety percent of the time in a Baccarat room. Baccarat stays busy enough without them.

The other ten percent of the time? All I can say is that no woman in the world could lure me into gambling if I didn't want to on a particular night. And the same should go for anyone with the common sense to know that the only reason you should sit down and gamble is if you want to enjoy yourself at a game. Or if you have that inexplicable feeling that tonight is going to be your lucky night.

Chapter

Five

I HAVE WATCHED BACCARAT PLAYED FOR SO LONG that someone once figured out that I had observed and presided over literally ten to twenty million separate decisions!

Out of it all has come a peculiar radar system for me. Invariably I can tell when a player sits down—after only a hand or two—whether he'll be a winner or a loser for the evening. Now, the odd part is that my feeling has nothing to do with whether or not he has won or lost that first wager or two. It is just something about his approach to the table and to the game. I have been wrong on occasion. But I have been right so often that it is eerie.

Sometimes, in the middle of the game, though nothing has been changed in the way a streak is going, I'll get a feeling that a "reverse" has taken place.

For example, a player I know will sit down and I'll sense that he's a loser for the night. Sure enough, he'll gradually fall into a losing run.

Suddenly, although he is still losing, something in his attitude changes and I know he'll end up a winner. Sure enough, time and time again, events bear me out. It's a little uncanny.

But then, that is one of the lures of gambling—that strange twist of fate that says if a man sat down thirty seconds sooner—a man, for example, who bets maximum money on bank when he holds the shoe—he might have won instead of lost $30,000 for the evening.

If there's one thing I've learned about gambling it's to recognize and respect streaks. This is true, incidentally, in all casino games.

If, for example, the cards favor the player for three consecutive decisions, then your next bet should either be player or you shouldn't bet at all! If you lose, you lose only one wager. If you bet against the trend, you can be suckered into betting and betting and betting. I've seen more fortunes lost by people who became emotionally committed to one position that went against the trend than through any other folly in gaming!

The fact that red has come up three times does

not in theory affect the next spin of the roulette wheel. But there are many who will then bet black, certain that it is now black's turn. Red can come up three more times or thirty more times.

To repeat, *because this is so important,* don't buck a trend. Either swing over or don't wager. I consider three or more decisions in one direction enough to be considered a trend.

Everyone in Vegas knows stories of gambler's lucky streaks. Here are two that I can vouch for.

A fellow, often in the news, was at the airport with friends, about to fly back to New York. The TWA clerk told him the flight was full and one of the people in his party hadn't had her ticket reconfirmed. The fellow hadn't slept all night—he never did on his final night in Vegas. But she had a husband and children to return to. Heroically, he gave up his seat, but jestingly warned the ticket agent that he would expect the bulkhead seat in First Class on the following morning.

His bags were packed and on the plane. Even his jacket was in his luggage. His friends tried to dissuade him but he assured them, "Look, it's okay. I feel lucky now."

They were skeptical—and with good reason. He had already dropped cash or signed markers for something approaching $50,000.

Away they went. Back to National Car Rental

he went. He retreived his rented car and headed
back to town.

He was so tired that he neglected to make the
left turn on Tropicana Road. Instead he found
himself dangerously sleepy at the wheel and approaching the International (now the Hilton).

He parked and wandered into the Baccarat
section. Two tables were operating. He sat down
at one. Just as he had been unlucky before, now
he became so lucky that he could do no wrong.

But he was also so tired that at one point he
opened his eyes and said, "What happened?"

"You just won $1,500," the croupier said.

He knew he needed sleep. But by now he was a
little paranoiac. He didn't know the hotel so he
didn't trust it. He had fistfuls of money and no
place to pocket it.

With security guards tailing him, he made his
way to the car. Somehow he found his way to The
Sands. He put most of the cash in a box in the
cashier's cage—asked for and got a room—and
went up to sleep.

Six hours later, refreshed, he began a tour of the
casinos where he had lost his money. Sometimes
he won and sometimes he lost but he won more
often than he lost.

By nine A.M. the next morning, he had recouped
his losses and had recovered and torn up his markers. In addition, he had a plastic bag full of $100

bills! It was the bag hotels sometimes provide as a courtesy for your wet washcloth!

When he approached the TWA counter, he kissed the agent on the cheek and handed him a $100 chip.

"This is because you bumped me off the flight yesterday."

Only after the plane took off did he count his money before the eyes of the startled stewardesses. He had won back his losses and $53,000 plus as well!

Here is another true story and although he doesn't want his name mentioned, this player agreed to tell it in his own words.

His story:

"I was really sour. I sat at the Baccarat table at the Aladdin and I couldn't win two wagers in a row.

"Earlier in the day, I had signed an $18,000 marker at the crap table. Unfortunately, I had a 'sky's the limit' credit rating at this particular place because I had applied for the right to buy some points in it—so they knew every legal dollar I owned.

"There was only one real player at the table—a big fellow with glasses who sat at the opposite side of the table. The others were shills.

"I kept betting against him, and of course I kept losing. Soon I had lost $20,000 at the table. I owed

$38,000. This was *big* money for the Aladdin in those days—and probably still is.

"I had nothing against the guy I was betting against. It's just the position I had taken. Incredibly often, he beat me by one point. He'd win $20 and I'd lose $2,000.

" 'Great!' I said sarcastically on one occasion.

" 'I don't feel so good about winning when I see how much you're losing,' he called across to me.

"That was surprising. Gamblers are usually self-concerned and this was a touch of humanity I hadn't expected.

"I called for $2,000 more. Manager Gil Gilbert nodded his okay. Ronald Steinman, who was running the game, pushed four white chips to me.

" 'Give me currency,' I said. 'And Gil—don't give me any more because if you do, I don't pay for it.'

"That's fair warning to a casino. If they're out to stretch and break you, they are on notice. Gil knew that I would make good the $40,000—but not a penny more.

"It was still early in the evening. I wasn't interested in girls or shows or drinking. I could make my usual bet and when I lost, I was through gambling for the night.

"I decided to extend the torture. The shoe had just moved to the real player at the end of the table. His money was on bank. I put $300 on player.

" 'Why don't you go with me just once?' he asked. It was almost a plea.

" 'Why? Do you feel lucky?'

" 'I'm going to make four passes,' he said.

" 'What the hell,' I thought to myself, 'why extend the agony another ten minutes?'

" 'Okay, I'm with you,' I said. I pushed the $300 to bank and piled the other $1,700 on top of it.

"He made three passes. Then he dealt a tie. I had one of those stomach hunches. 'Nothing personal,' I said, and switched bets. I was right. From then on, I could do no wrong. We'd shout to each other, 'What are you gonna do?' and agree on a simultaneous position.

"In a while I requested my marker. It was at about this time that Gil whispered something into the other player's ear. I leaped up and ran to his side of the table.

" 'What is it, Gil?' I asked.

" 'Nothing, Mr. S. It's just that we thought the gentleman might have been bothering you.'

" 'Bothering me?' I said. 'Next to my wife and children he's the dearest friend I have in the world!'

" 'You make all the noise you want,' I told him.

"When I decided to cash in, I had not only recouped the entire $40,000 but I was ahead $6,000. I watched while they counted out the stacks of hundreds in exchange for the five hundred dollar

73

chips. When I looked up, the other player had vanished. He hadn't even waited for me to thank him!

"Some months later I ran into him again in a casino. 'What happened to you that night?' I asked. 'Where did you disappear to?'

" 'I didn't want to bother you,' he said.

"Remember now, his plaintive 'why don't you go with me just once' meant the difference between losing forty grand and winning $6,000—and was the start of an $84,000 turnaround!"

You'll hear lots of stories like that in Vegas—and most of them are true.

And it's that mystical thing about gambling—the sudden twist when the gods smile where they had been frowning—that makes gambling the only business I'd want to be part of!

Chapter

Six

IF YOU REALLY WANT TO KNOW THE TRUTH, THERE are no "secrets" about professional gambling, any more than there are about tennis. There are a lot of things people have yet to learn about either pastime. But that doesn't make them secrets. They are just "facts of life" that many participants don't know or never spend the time to discover.

When it comes to gambling the way professionals do, there are only three basic ingredients: knowledge, acquired skill and money management. Oh, there are a lot of little things to learn, things that time and experience will tell you. Most of these important secondary gambling adages are no more than common sense.

For example, gamble when you are well rested, and when nothing negative can cloud your mind and affect your perception, analysis and decision making. Being tired or upset when you play doesn't mean that you have to lose, but it sure helps!

I don't think anyone should gamble who is afraid of losing. It's obvious that when your confidence is shaky your performance will be bad.

To gamble, you don't have to begin with a lot of money, but you certainly need some nerve and some courage. Because effective gambling, like accomplished skiing, sometimes requires you to go against some very strong instincts.

One of the basic rules of skiing, for example, is to keep all your weight over the downhill ski, the one closest to the direction in which you can take the worst falls. Now if you were standing on the edge of a cliff and you did that, you'd be increasing your chances of a grisly, premature death. But in skiing it works just the other way. It's a matter of weight. Don't ask me to explain it. Any dashing young ski instructor can do that for you. Just take my word that it works. By keeping your weight on that downhill ski, you actually decrease the chances of falling.

In gambling, the key is to control your losses and capitalize on winning streaks. In other words, to lose as little as possible and win as much as possible. There are ways to accomplish this. Every professional knows these principles.

Simply stated, they consist of (1) keeping to a

low average bet while you are losing and (2) doubling up almost everytime you win.

Most people do just the opposite, doubling up when they are losing in a foolish attempt to get their losses back fast, and restricting themselves by becoming conservative when they begin to win. It's the old story of self-preservation. They lose and they think they must get back to a break-even point as quickly as possible. So they double up before coming into a win pattern, and what happens?

If a man has lost three of four $10 bets in a row and then begins doubling up on each of five subsequent losing bets, he will blow a total of $620 trying to get back $30 or $40. Even if he only bets three times, if he doubles up each time to try to get his $30 or $40 back, he loses $20 more, then $40 more, then $80 more—a total of $140 to recoup his lost $30 or $40. And that means a grand total of $170 or $180 lost. Most amateur or occasional gamblers will quit at this point, or well before it, out even more money than they originally lost because they did not follow or were unaware of the professional principle that applies to losing streaks, or patterns.

Now there are a lot of fancy systems people gamble by—none of which, by the way, is given even a second thought by professionals. One of them, used by many experienced pleasure gamblers, goes diametrically against the professional principle that applies to losing patterns. It works this way: You place a bet. When you lose, you double up. If you lose again you double up again, and so on, continuing to double up after each losing bet until you win. So what does it get you? In the end—figure it out—you wind up winning an amount equal to your original bet after risking increasingly larger sums. And you are *risking* them all right.

Suppose your first bet is the lowest Baccarat minimum in Vegas—$5. You use this principle and lose your first four bets, which means, after doubling up, that you are out $75 ($5+$10+$20+ $40). So you double up on your fifth bet and wager $80. You win and get back $80—$5 more than you have already lost. Fine. You are $5 ahead but you have had a lot of worry and sweat for it. And the sweat was justified, because runs of six, seven or eight passes in Baccarat are not uncommon. There are many runs of nine to twelve passes. And sometimes they run as high as eighteen or twenty. Supposing you were betting that double-up business when you were losing and the decisions went against you nine times in a row? Do you know how much you'd be out? $2,555!

There is one instance, in one game—craps— when this system might work for what a professional would call minimal gain. That's when the players at the crap table are experiencing an indiscriminate win and loss pattern. In other words, no one is holding the dice for more than two, three or four rolls. It follows then that if you are doubling up while betting the "Don't Pass" line, *against each shooter on every roll,* they can win two, three or four in a row and then, by doubling up your bets after each loss you will win back your original bet each time a shooter loses the dice.

So your original bet is $5 and there are ten shooters at the table. That means when the dice have made a complete circle of the table, you will come out ahead $50—$5 for each player. Just remember, however, that every time you attempt it, you may suddenly be up against a fantastically hot shooter. I've seen a dollar bettor roll two dozen passes in a row. If you happen to come up against somebody who rolls even twelve passes in a row, you better have an enormous bankroll—not to mention genitals made of brass—to ride the roll out until Mr. Lucky loses. And even then, remember that all you are going to come out ahead with is the amount of your original bet. Is it worth risking all that cash for so measly a return?

Even more of a strain on your courage is following the professional principle that applies to winning. As I've indicated, people win a little and walk out of the casino never realizing that they could have won much more. Players hit a winning streak and what do they do? They bet the same amount or maybe a little more each time they win. A professional gambler rides his luck when he is winning. But you'll never see a professional bet the same amount consistently when he's winning —unless its the house limit.

By knowledge, I don't mean familiarity with the composition of moon rocks. Or the ability to recite the Bible Chapter and Verse. What we are talking about here is knowledge of each of the games you get involved in—the rules and how to play.

You can sit down and read all you want about poker, blackjack, craps, roulette, any game you care to mention, but you won't really have a knowledge of the game until you actually play it. So my first suggestion, if you have never played a game before, is to try it at home with your wife, girlfriend, son or daughter. After reading the rules of the game at the library, play a little. For matches, toothpicks, chips, whatever you care to. But *play*.

You don't necessarily have to buy books on gambling games. Your library has plenty of them. There are dozens of gambling titles for you to choose from, most of which will lay the rules of all the games out for you. So I won't go into the rules of every game for you here. There's no need to when so many others have done it before me. But to give you some idea of what I mean by knowledge, let me cite a few facts concerning blackjack and craps.

Common sense will tell you that before you play craps you should know not only how the game is played but what the proper odds are on each bet, and what the *real* odds against you winning a bet are compared to the odds the house will actually pay off if you win. (What the house pays in craps is generally spelled out right on the table itself. And if you are puzzled or making a bet where the odds aren't posted right out on the green felt, any house man at the table will gladly tell you if you ask.) By all means, you should be aware of what the proper payoffs are. No one in Vegas will cheat you intentionally, but where human beings are involved, mistakes can be made.

There is more to know about craps, much more, than the fact that you get $5 from the casino when you bet $5 and make either a seven or eleven on your first toss, or your point on a subsequent roll.

You should know, for example, that the house has a hidden percentage in the "even money" bets a player makes on the Pass line and Don't Pass line. And that by making a free odds bet behind either the Pass line or Don't Pass line, after the shooter has rolled a point and is about to try to duplicate it, you can reduce the hidden percentage to a point where you have *just about* an actual even money wager going for you.

There are other facts about playing craps that are, shall we say, useful to know. Amateurs make casinos rich by betting the hard numbers (2+2, 3+3, 4+4, 5+5), all of which have the warning signal in the high odds payoff attached to them right there on the table.

Sure, I've known someone who occasionally began to bet 2 or 12 and who is a pro. But do you think he did it on a hunch? Nothing doing. He would stand at a table with a little counter in his pocket on which he would register every roll of the dice, keeping his eye on those particular numbers. When, for example, 2 or 12 didn't come up in their natural probability range of once in thirty-six times, he'd keep counting. If they didn't come up in 144 rolls or only came up once in that many, he'd begin making the proposition bet that pays thirty to one. (Don't be fooled by the language "thirty-one *for* one." That includes your original bet!)

He'd stick with it and then, every thirty rolls or so that it still hadn't appeared, he'd increase his bet.

He had patience. And he wasn't playing games: he was there to take money from the table.

The average person has neither the iron fortitude nor the cold mathematical understanding of odds to be willing to put that much effort into getting the odds seemingly on your side. And mark you, I said "seemingly" for there is no guarantee that the 2 or 12 would *ever* come up!

Baccarat is your best percentage wager in a casino. But it is so fast that the pace makes up for the small odds against you.

Dice odds are 1.41 against you on the clean (Pass line) wager.

Either of those games are money games for me.

Roulette? Pure luck. When you sit down, consider that you are buying lottery tickets or making a contribution for the pretty surroundings.

Blackjack is the most dangerous game in a casino. It looks and seems simple. There are books that tell you how to "count" fives or pictures and "beat" the house. If it was all that easy, the authors would be beating the house rather than writing books.

The fact is that although there is an alleged percentage against the player, this percentage *is a deceptive illusion*.

With every roll of the dice, the odds against you are the same. But with every card dealt from a blackjack deck, *the odds change!*

Unless you're another Einstein with a fantastic memory and a computer mind, keep away from blackjack except as a relaxing entertainment. It doesn't take a giant brain to understand why casinos have so many blackjack tables and why these are so comfortable! You sit down. Free cigarettes and cigars. Free drinks. The longer you sit, the more unlikely you'll stand up a winner.

We pros have a saying that "even the house doesn't know how good the percentage is going for it in blackjack." Believe me that profits are fabulous. Most players get ground out. Winners? I've yet to hear of one bidding for the casino because of the size of his winnings!

I've given it to you as straight as if I were your father and you were my son. Whether you take my advice is now your concern!

Chapter

Seven

THERE IS A SUBTLE SKILL TO BE ACQUIRED IF YOU gamble with any regularity: the ability to read patterns. Anyone reading this book should already be aware that wins and losses tend to go in streaks, or, as a professional gambler would describe them, drifts. And there are separate patterns for every game in a casino, each particular table, and for each individual player—yourself soon to be one of them —at any moment of a given gambling day.

This is one facet of gambling knowledge that can be turned into a skill—the ability to read those patterns to your advantage. But it could take an enormous investment of time, study, and, unfortunately, money. Because before you develop the skill, you will be at a slight disadvantage in any game you play.

Knowing how to read patterns will tell you when

to play and when not to, when you should bet with another player or with the house, and when you are headed into an individual, personal, loss or win pattern yourself.

When I'm ready to gamble, I usually walk up to a table and watch ten or fifteen decisions before I bet a nickel. That way I catch the drift a little and see whether the house is winning more than the players during this particular part of a long-term pattern. It's like reading a graph, in a way. You know before you look at the graph that there will be upward and downward swings.

In gambling, an upward swing for the house means a corresponding downward swing for the players. Those swings, or arcs, in the graph can be profitable if you read them right. You may, for example, come in and read—accurately—a winning drift for the players and start betting with them. But you may have read it just before it starts the other way. So, you have to be cool and alert.

Staying on top of the pattern after you've started to play will indicate drift shifts that should dictate a change in your own betting pattern. You read a pattern that spells: Players Are Winning More Than The House. You bet with the players for awhile, but as you are betting, you notice that after five or six decisions the pattern starts to change. So you begin betting against the players and with the house.

The patterns I'm talking about are sometimes a lot less than obvious. They're most easily recognizable when a lot of people at a particular table are winning. During a crowded weekend for example. When the players *aren't* winning, nobody takes much notice. Nor do they realize that definite patterns are in action when only a few people are playing. It just isn't as easy to read these drifts when nobody is excited and shouting about what is happening. So you have to keep track even more carefully during the quiet times.

I've seen the player's hand or the banker's hand make as high as twenty passes at times, and nobody noticed it because few people were betting the right way and winning.

I've seen cases where a house was going sour for a long period of time in one particular game. In one instance it was Baccarat, and the casino losing pattern extended, with occasional swings up into brief periods of winning, for almost a year. Now any gambler really observing that game with any sense about him would be aware of the losing house pattern and would try to take advantage of it.

Unless you observe a game carefully, you can sometimes be trapped into believing that something happens more often than not, simply because you have observed it. In Baccarat, for example, I have noticed on many, many occasions that tie hands seem to follow one another in bursts of two, three and four. Four ties in a row. I can't tell you how many times I've seen that. But in a case like this, you have to call on your common sense and your knowledge of probabilities.

There is no known reason in the world why tie hands should come in bunches, or sequences. I'm sure that my observation, therefore, has been distorted by the fact that I just haven't noticed many tie hands that come along by themselves. And by the fact that sequences of tie hands are much more noticeable than individual ties. The point, of course, is that your faculties can deceive you—unless you question and analyze everything you believe to be a pattern.

Even in Baccarat, where no knowledge of the game is necessary to play, the ability to read patterns helps. It isn't absolutely necessary if you are willing to rely solely on luck. But your luck—and your winnings—will increase sharply *in any game* if you know—through pattern reading—when to take advantage of a win drift.

If you are ever to have even a remote chance of walking away a winner more than occasionally, you must practice what professionals call "money management."

In this case, money management has nothing to do with the way you balance your checkbook or whether you are always in a position to pay your bills on time. The manipulative money management I'm talking about has to do solely with the money you gamble with on any given occasion.

Professional gamblers have a saying: "Always try to get the strength out of your money." By that they mean betting in a way that will reduce your losses and put you in the position to win.

Now let me say right out front that I have lost—and lost big—many times while following the principles I am about to repeat and explain for you. On any given night or over any given stretch of time, Lady Luck—like Mother Nature in that television ad for margarine—can suddenly or gradually strand you in a blizzard of misfortune. Sometimes the cards and the dice just won't go your way no matter what you do. But in the long run, these principles of money management—which I consider the most important "secrets" of gambling— have worked for me. They will work for you.

The objectives of the philosophy are rather simple and to the point. Objective Number One is, as I've said, to control your losses while you are losing so that you have a chance to last out your unlucky drift and take advantage of a subsequent win pattern.

Objective Number Two: To win more than the amount of money you start gambling with, possibly many times more, if you are winning—and to break even or stay ahead if you lose more decisions than you win on a given night.

Sounds acceptable, doesn't it? And all you have to do to reach these two goals is:

1) Stick to a low average bet when you are losing, and . . .

2) Increase your wagers as soon as a winning trend is indicated.

Every professional I have ever known has followed these principles strictly. Yet few amateur or casual gamblers do. Why, I'll never know. People read up on, investigate, learn about and try to apply professional principles to everything they do from cooking to sex. With the exception of gambling. In gambling, amateurs tend to remain amateurs, though they obviously don't have to.

Chapter

Eight

I'VE BEEN TALKING ABOUT THE PROFESSIONAL'S philosophy of gambling—particularly the way we follow the winning principle in its purest form. Now I'm going to take you into Baccarat and show you how I apply that same principle in both its pure form and a few variations. After that, I'll try to point out a wrinkle or two in the philosophy that will be of some use to the average, weekend gambler.

If I've got a thousand dollars to bet and I've just sat down at a Baccarat table, here's the way I would manage my money: I would bet a hundred dollars at a time— sticking to the low average of one tenth to one twentieth of my stake if I'm just beginning or in a losing pattern—until I won two or preferably three wagers in a row. Now I double my bet to $200. If I win again, I might add $100 to it to make a $300 bet.

Sounds simple, doesn't it? Even if I lose more bets than I win—I will walk away a winner. Because the amount of each losing bet will tend to be small and the winner bet larger.

In most cases, when I'm gambling, I will stop for a break, have a cup of coffee and make sure that I know exactly where I'm at.

Now if I'm losing, while playing with an original $1,000 stake, I try to do exactly what the losing pattern principle tells me to: I make low average bets of $100, then if I slip down to a $400 to $500 bankroll, I drop down to a $50 average bet, then to a $35, then maybe $25, and then to the house minimum of $20. (I don't usually play in the few places where they have $5 minimums.) That way I get anywhere from fifteen to twenty chances to begin winning again.

Whenever I start to win, even if I'm down to my last $100, my last $40, I start increasing, because I know that I can get back to my original position or better very quickly by doing that.

Sometimes the cards are so bad I end up losing everything. But that doesn't happen often. It usually takes quite a bit of time for a game to take all my money away. Because on all but the very worst nights—when, by the way, I will read the patterns and maybe just decide to quit when I'm halfway down through my bankroll—I'm bound to pick up a win drift or two during those fifteen to twenty-five decisions I guarantee myself.

It's true that sometimes all the win drifts—the short ones—do is delay the time it takes to lose everything. But for as many times as that happens, there are as many or more instances when the win drifts are long enough to put me ahead. Then I take stock and start all over again.

I've been talking about the rough nights. The good ones are when you can't seem to do anything wrong and everything you do clicks just right.

By the way, if you want to see the converse of this principle, watch someone who bets consistently no matter what. Watch a $20 bettor receive the shoe and make eight passes. He's delighted with himself when it's over. He has never wagered more than $20 at a time and he has a profit of $140.

Now, if he had played my system most conservatively, his wagers would have been $20, $20, $30, $40, $50, $60, $70, $80, $90.

He would have lost that last $90 wager.

But instead of winning $140, he would have been ahead $370. And at no time from the third wager on, could a losing hand have kept him from remaining a winner for the series.

On the other hand, if one really feels lucky and feels that a streak has begun, he could wager $20, $20, $30, $50, $90, $160, $250, $300, $400. This is still wagering so that if he lost on any decision after the second, he would have profits. Yet for exactly the same number of wins as the first player who ended up $140 ahead, this player ends up $920 ahead.

Same $20 bet to begin with. Same number of winning hands.

Beginning to see the light?

It's a little like poker. A good player can sit at a table all night with the most atrocious cards and end up losing a few hundred dollars while a bad player with the same hands will lose thousands.

A good player with good cards can win thousands while a bad player with the same hands will only win hundreds.

Next to "luck", money management is the most important feature of any gaming session. Never forget that for an instant.

A big question in gambling is "When do you stop?"

You have to avoid the trap of continuing to gamble too long. Set your own loss limit. It could be when you get down to one half or one quarter of your bankroll. It could be all of it. That's got to be up to you. Just be wary of getting down to the bottom of your bankroll—the amount you have decided to gamble with in the first place—and then dipping beyond it into other funds. More often than not, those funds are going to be needed for other things, necessities. And when you begin playing with that sort of money, chances are you are also beginning to play with fire.

When do you quit when you are winning? That also depends on the individual gambler. Much of the decision will depend on whether or not you still feel lucky. Winning can affect the way you are playing. You may no longer be in total control —and that will be enough to tell you to quit. But a lot of it will depend on how much you have set out to win.

There is a casino saying, "Don't go for the chandeliers."

Okay. But when to stop? I think the time is when you begin to feel like stopping—if you're still winning, you play with a control in mind.

"The next two bets I lose, I quit."

Or even, "The first bet I lose, I quit."

But if you make this mental decision, stick to it. Don't get sucked into a losing quagmire that will gobble back all of your winnings. You'll hate yourself if you do.

If your win goal is high, and you don't seem to quite reach it, check your overall pattern and ask yourself if it indicates that your luck seems to be limited to a less modest gain. If so, maybe you should quit *now* and not try to reach your high goal.

A lot of people set win goals for themselves, just as they set artificial bet limits in order to take money back into their bankroll automatically after anything from three to six consecutive wins. There's nothing wrong with asking yourself before you begin gambling: "What amount of winning is going to satisfy me?" After all, you've set a limit for losses, haven't you?

By far, in my book, the most important thing to consider with regard to quitting while you're ahead is whether or not you are really on a long, lucky streak. If you keep winning, despite a few reversals, and you keep adding money to your bankroll, I would say keep playing. Take advantage of the fact that you are lucky on a particular night. God knows, there will be lots of nights when you won't be lucky, so why not make up for them while the pattern is in your favor? If your head has remained cool and you are able to keep the principles in mind and apply them, stick to it until the pattern indicates that your luck is reversing. You'll never know if that sign is accurate, but that fact is a lot easier to live with if you've quit while you're way ahead rather than far behind.

Once in awhile, a pro will go into a game with $1,000 and on a hunch—remember that a professional's instinct can often be more than intuition

—he may bet $500 or the whole $1,000. I've done it, because something told me I was going to hit the first one and then two or three more. That's why gambling is our life, because we are drawn into those situations more than other people are. But for the most part, and this is especially true for the casual gambler, the principles, the philosophy I've set down in this book are the ones that over an hour, a day, or a year, will give you the best possibility of winning.

And if you lose? Keep accurate records so that you know what your overall balance is. Each gamble is a new gamble. Each game is a new game. And if you carry a losing attitude into the casino the next time you play, you will certainly lose again.

And this should give you something to think about. The next time you are about to enter a casino, ask yourself, "Do I really *want* to win?"

A silly question? Think about it.

Many people gamble to lose because they lack self-esteem. Or because they want to atone for guilt. Or for a variety of psychological reasons. These are all an extra edge for the house.

How many times have you seen someone who seemed terribly uncomfortable as he won and won and won. Finally, he loses, and a look of great relief appears on his face as he walks from the table.

There are deeper than obvious reasons for the common use of the expression "I took a bath" in response to "How'd you do?".

If you want to take a bath, do it in your tub at home.

If you want to gamble, do it to win.

Chapter

Nine

THE VERSION OF BACCARAT I BROUGHT WITH ME from Cuba is played in Las Vegas, a few places in England and Europe and at many South American casinos. Since most readers of this book are probably going to gamble primarily in Vegas, I'll concentrate on that city. The Las Vegas Strip runs north and south, with the city itself sitting on the northern end. Working from the southernmost end of The Strip towards town, Baccarat is offered in the following places:

THE TROPICANA

Baccarat has been added within the last year at the Tropicana. The minimum bet is $5 unless the casino is exceptionally busy. Then the minimum is raised to $20. The Tropicana's maximum bet or limit is $2,000. The Baccarat table is set out in the middle of the casino, surrounded by all the other games. One table.

THE DUNES

Minimum $20, limit $2,000. Sometimes the Dunes extends its limit to $4,000. The Baccarat room in the recently redecorated casino is in good taste, sunken about a foot below the casino and off to one side by itself. It's a beautifully appointed area. Good atmosphere, plenty of space, just what a Baccarat room should be. One table.

CAESAR'S PALACE

Minimum usually $20, but as high as $100 during busier times. The house limit in Baccarat is generally $2,000, but they will lift it to $4,000 and possibly more for some high rollers. The atmosphere at Caesar's is wonderful. It's a nicely appointed room on a level a little higher than the casino. The room is situated off to the left of the showroom. A standard of elegance that the game of Baccarat calls for and deserves. One table generally, often two.

THE FLAMINGO

Minimum $20, occasionally, $5. Limit invariably $2,000. A casual, adequate room for players who do not demand a high standard of elegance.

THE SANDS

The first hotel in Vegas to offer Baccarat. Minimum $20. Limit $2,000 without exception. The room is off to the right of the crap tables and the entrance to the showroom. Fairly well decorated, comfortable. One table.

THE FRONTIER

Minimum $20, occasionally lowered to $5. Limit $2,000 without exception. The Frontier Baccarat room is comfortable enough, but it lacks the qualities of real elegance and privacy that a true Baccarat room should have.

THE DESERT INN

Minimum $20, but frequently as low as $5. Limit $2,000. A fairly small room on the left of the casino near the showroom. Nicely decorated and laid out. One table.

THE RIVIERA

Minimum $20, sometimes $5. Maximum $2,000, but occasionally more for some high rollers. A comfortable place to play. One table.

THE STARDUST

Minimum $5, up to $20 on busy nights. Maximum invariably $2,000. The room, reopened for the third time recently, is fenced off from the

Stardust casino near one of the establishment's restaurants. More than adequate for those who love Baccarat and don't mind very rudimentary decor.

THE SAHARA

Minimum $20, occasionally $5. Limit $2,000. A small room that is almost as elegant as the Baccarat areas at Caesar's and The Dunes. One table.

THE HILTON INTERNATIONAL

Minimum $20. Maximum $2,000. This hotel is actually located a block east of The Strip. The Hilton International has a sunken Baccarat room similar in design to the one at the Dunes. It is as spacious, handsomely decorated and elegant as any room in Vegas. One table, frequently two.

THE MINT

Minimum $5. Limit $500. The Mint is located in downtown Las Vegas rather than on The Strip itself. The Baccarat area is located in the middle of the casino. Pretty, but not as private or sedate a setting as The Dunes, The Sands, Caesar's Palace or The Hilton International. The lowest limit in Las Vegas. One table.

THE UNION PLAZA

Minimum $5. Limit $2,000. Neither figure ever

changes at this downtown hotel. The room is bright and comfortable, but situated right in the middle of the casino. It's roped off, but for some people, the noise from the casino games might be distracting. Not an elegant room, but here, as well as at The Mint, the casual gambler can play Baccarat according to professional principles anytime with a lot less money. One table.

Those hotels and casinos in Las Vegas that do offer Baccarat generally keep the game open from early evening to three, four or five in the morning. Some hotels run Baccarat games during the day on weekends only. Caesar's Palace and The Hilton International are the only hotels that currently offer Baccarat twenty-four hours a day.

Chapter

Ten

PEOPLE GAMBLE FOR ALL SORTS OF REASONS. SOME use it as an emotional cleanser. Others play for the excitement. And, as I've pointed out, not everyone plays to win—though people sometimes want to believe they want to win. Gaming offers many people a way to entertain themselves, relax. It can be an enjoyable diversion if you are careful with it, just the way fire can be warming when it is kept under control. Gambling can take your mind off other things. It can also provide you with thrills.

Gambling has always been the source of great enjoyment for me, and it can be for you if you heed a little advice:

Never gamble with money you can't afford to lose. Set a loss limit for yourself and don't go below it.

Gamble for enjoyment, but remember that you will enjoy it more if you have the knowledge and skills most games require, and you learn and stick to professional principles of betting.

Know when to quit.

Drink if it will help you enjoy yourself when you're gambling, but don't drink so much that it cuts into your ability to think, analyze patterns, manage money and make fast decisions with a clear head. Keep in mind that some of the smartest gamblers around will never touch a drink while they are in action.

And if things go really bad with you, you might recall this story that songwriter Irving Caesar tells about Nick the Greek.

The Greek was in a private game on the second floor of a house where the host was throwing a very plush party.

When the game ended, the Greek had dropped about $240,000.

Everybody left the room to join the festivities except Irving Caesar, who sat stunned on the edge of the bed. Irving hadn't played, he'd just watched. But the knowledge that his friend had lost all that money was overwhelming.

Eventually, he made his way slowly down the

stairs. There, before his disbelieving eyes, was Nick the Greek in the middle of the dance floor, dancing and singing with delight.

At the end of the dance he saw Irving and came over to him concerned. "Caesar, you look sick. Are you all right?"

"Nick!" Irving Caesar said. "Nick! How can you sing and dance? You just lost nearly a quarter of a million dollars upstairs!"

Nick the Greek smiled at his songwriter friend. "But Irving—your life doesn't go with it!"

They say that Lady Luck gets tired of carrying anyone on her shoulders for too long, but that, in time, she'll give everyone a lift or two. Your lucky turn will come, and when it does, enjoy every minute of it. I hope that I have shown you how to entice her your way a little sooner and to have a little more to show for it when she drops you than you would otherwise have had.

And remember, your life doesn't go with it!

Good luck!